*Knowing and Drawing*

# TREES

BOOK II

---

*written and illustrated by*

ADRIAN HILL

LONDON

BLANDFORD PRESS

FOR

LUKE AND VERA

WITH

AFFECTION

*First published in 1960*
*Second edition 1969*


*Printed and bound in Great Britain by*
*Jarrold and Sons Ltd, Norwich*

# Contents

*Fig. 1. Right shape*

# Introduction

IT is one thing to learn to recognize trees, and even to become proficient at drawing them—and I have touched on these points in the companion book—but I would like to say a little here about how to introduce them into your picture.

Once you know something of the individual characteristics of shape and growth of your tree models, you must see that they occupy the right position and cover the required area in your chosen compositions. Obvious faults can often be seen when, for instance, vertical tree subjects are cut down to fit them into horizontal designs. Compare Figs. 1 and 2, where height and dignity of the Beeches are impaired when only the lower portion of their trunks is included. Only by doing a rough can you decide which is the better shape for the height or width of your tree forms.

*Fig. 2. Wrong shape*

*Fig. 3. Wrong*

*Fig. 4. Right*

Conversely, the same error can be seen by comparing Figs. 3 and 4.

Another important factor, often forgotten, is the proper lighting of your subject. As a general rule I would say that side lighting is always preferable to painting with the light directly behind you or when painting into the sun. (*Contre le jour*, as the French describe it.)

Light implies shadows, and shadows can enrich foregrounds and give depth and mystery to foliage and play an important part in directing the eye or giving solidity to your trees. But shadows that stem directly and steeply *towards* the spectator (if you face the sun) or fall directly *behind* the trees (if you have the sun at your back), where they are lost to view, cannot do this.

Figs. 5, 6, and 7 will show you more clearly how side-lighting your subject will set off your shadows to the best advantage. It is therefore not just a matter of *where* you sit to paint, but *when* you judge the light most advantageous in bringing out the best pictorial results.

*Fig. 5. Light from left*

*Fig. 6. Facing the sun*

Foliage, especially for the beginner in watercolours, will always present difficulties. I would say that even the over-simplified form, where solid green shapes stand duty for leaves in mass, is more satisfactory than the overworked tree in which the leaves are seen as multiple separate details and are conscientiously painted in as such. The compromise is really a matter of touch, which in the practised hand can vary the texture of the painted areas, combining by the use of broad washes of colour for the density of foliage in shadow, with a more flexible and crisp handling where small clusters of leaves catch the light. And, of course, only continual practice and experiment can achieve the desired effect.

Whether you are painting in oils or watercolours the time-honoured practice of looking at your subject through half-closed

*Fig. 7. Sun directly behind*

eyes will readily disclose where detail disappears and where it remains visible. Other examples of tree compositions included here indicate the importance of the time of year as well as time of day you decide to paint your picture.

Finally, charcoal, especially now it is made up in pencil form, is excellent both for making tree studies and for drawing in your tree-forms before painting.

The illustrations on pages 10, 11 and 12 have been taken from leaves in my sketch-books and show studies of:

Tree Constructions (2 drawings of an Umbrella Oak).

Tree Comparisons (street trees and garden trees).

Tree Compositions (in the countryside).

*Umbrella Oak in full leaf*

*The dry tree*

*Chestnuts in North Street, Midhurst*

*In a Midhurst garden*

*Cornish Lane*

*Farm entrance*

# *The Wellingtonia*

HISTORY

Few trees can boast such a romantic history as the Wellingtonia, although it is less than 100 years since it was first introduced into Britain. We read that a certain General Bidwell first discovered it in North America in 1841, and having learnt some facts about its incredible proportions brought it over here. Referred to as the 'Big Tree', it was decided to christen it Wellingtonia, as a mark of respect to England's greatest soldier, the Duke of Wellington. As the tree, however, had originally been found in America, our American cousins took exception to this and named it the Washingtonia after *their* most distinguished citizen, George Washington! Twelve years after the discovery, J. D. Matthews collected seeds from Calaveras Grove and sent them back to Great Britain, where they were distributed. Today the Wellingtonia is a distinguished landmark in parks and botanical gardens throughout the country. Along the Pacific coast of America, trees are still flourishing which the experts agree must be over 4,000 years old. The age of the tallest and mightiest is estimated at about 4,250 years.

*Bole of Wellingtonia*

*The Wellingtonia*

*Leaves of Wellingtonia*

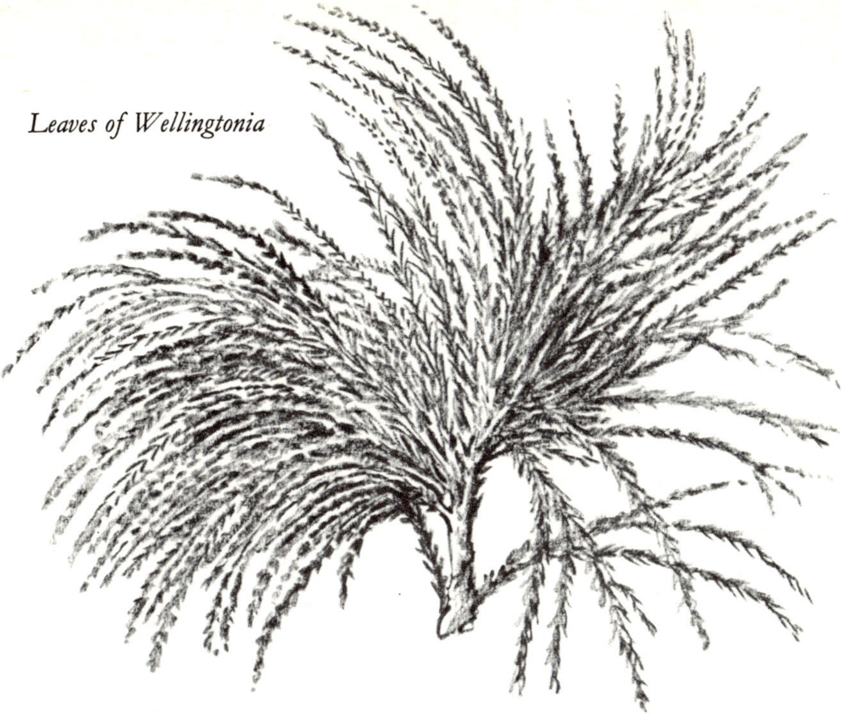

DESCRIPTION

The Wellingtonia is a close relation of the huge Redwood tree, and alongside it might almost be called a young brother. The tallest in the British Isles is possibly the one in County Wicklow, Ireland, which is—or was, a few years ago—143 feet tall with a girth of over 16 feet, 5 feet from the bole.

Being an evergreen, pyramid-shaped, and of such massive size, it is very easy to recognize. In fact, there is no conifer of such stature the least like it, and in any collection of forest trees the Wellingtonia is usually head and shoulders above the rest! And presuming that St Barbe Baker is correct when he states, 'No Redwood tree has ever been known to die of disease or old age' —the Wellingtonia is in for a long life!

Its great bole is covered with warm-tinted fibrous bark, and the mighty pendulous branches support compact tufted masses of dark grey-green 'leaves' which sometimes look almost blue. Together they form a tree of great dignity which dwarfs all our other ornamental trees.

The Wellingtonia, like such trees as the Normandy Poplar and Douglas Fir, is a gift to the painter of tree compositions. Because of its precise, perpendicular silhouette, it can always be safely introduced to act as a foil for the more numerous broad-leafed trees with their rounded heads. It responds equally well to pencil, pen, or brush, and to decorative or impressionistic treatment, for the foliage which is composed of massed needles can be depicted as well with precision as portrayed in broad, thick brush-strokes. It lends itself to the etcher's needle or to the tools of the wood engraver, and is equally at home when cast for a principal character as it is when acting as a background support for village church or other rural architecture.

*Symbol* *Pattern* *Outline* *Form*

*The Wellingtonia*

*Acacia* (see p. 17)

# *The Acacia*

HISTORY

The Acacia has an interesting history. It is a native of North America, where it is known as the Locust tree. The early missionaries gave it this name, believing that it was the fruit of this tree that sustained St John in the Wilderness. Although it had been grown in this country as an ornamental tree for nearly 200 years, it was not really established until William Cobbett reintroduced it as a timber tree on his return from America in 1820. It soon came to be in great demand and production at first could not keep pace. Although Cobbett's prediction that it would outstrip the Oak proved false, the evidence of his belief is seen in the number of these picturesque trees which grace so many gardens in London and in other parks throughout Britain.

*Bole of Acacia*

*Acacia*

*Leaves of Acacia*

DESCRIPTION

The Acacia has numerous individual characteristics and so is easily recognizable. Its trunk which is rarely upright takes on a slight slant. The mature bark has a unique tracery, heavily fissured as if cut by the hand of a wood engraver, the pattern of the trunk in some old trees delighting the eye by its fantastic engraved ornamentation. The branch formations resemble the pictorial symbol of forked lightning as they jerk their way spasmodically from the trunk to carry a wealth of delicate foliage which seems strangely at variance with the Gothic nature of the trunk. It can attain a height of over 70 feet.

It is a very late starter, the fairy-like leaves only making their appearance at the end of May or early June. These are long and narrow and are divided into a large number of short oval leaflets, reminiscent of feathers. The flowers are similar to those of the Laburnum, except that they are white and droop from the axils of the leaves in fragrant clusters. The contrast of colour between the dark wood and tender green of the foliage make the Acacia one of the most picturesque additions to our public parks and gardens.

Whether studied as a 'close-up' or portrayed as a full-length portrait, the Acacia makes a splendid model for both pencil and brush. It is full of good drawing in the configuration of trunk and pattern of branch formation. It combines an unusual blend of delicacy with strength, and age with innocence.

The tree readily discloses its framework of bough and branch, even in full leaf, except in the case of the young sapling. This means that its characteristic manner of growth is never completely obscured by a mass of foliage. The spaces between the outline of branch and leaf should be closely observed, as they are part of its personality.

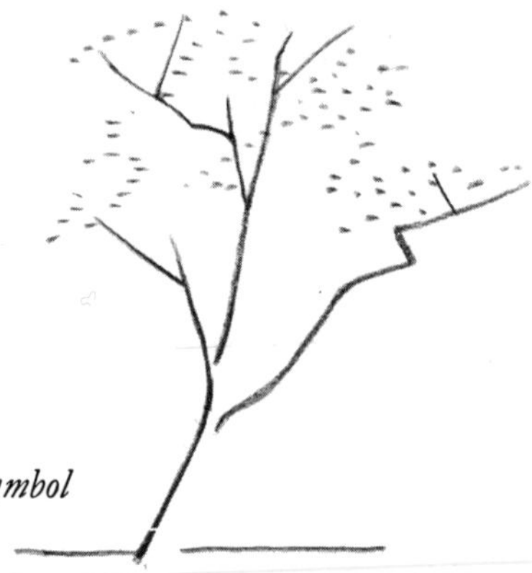

*Symbol*

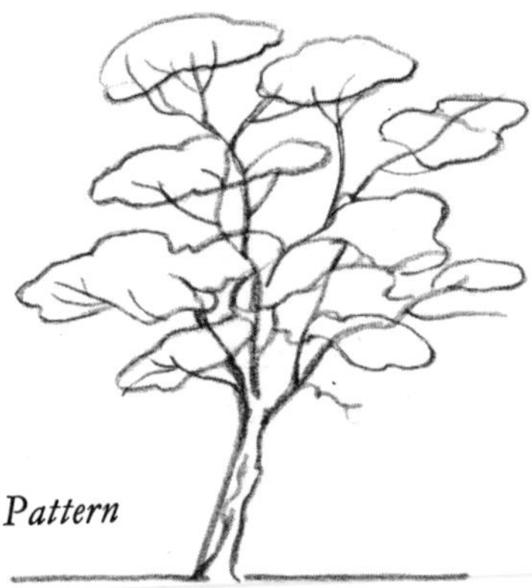

*Pattern*

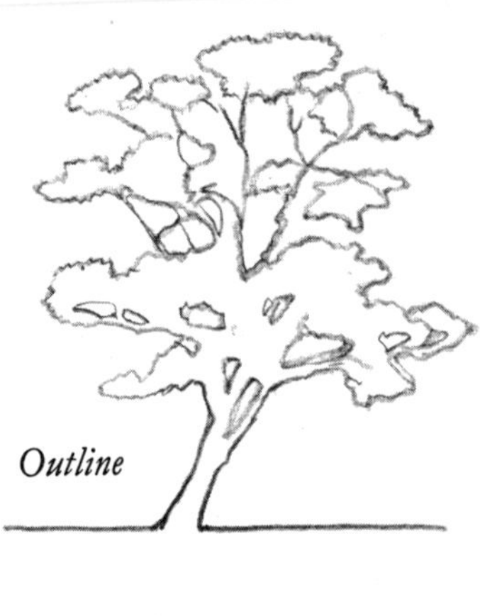

*Outline*

*Form*

# *The Ash*

HISTORY

The Ash can fairly claim a British birthright. While it has neither the majestic strength of the Oak nor the muscular elegance of the Beech, the Ash somehow combines the attributes of both without rivalling either in strength or beauty.

Superstition has always surrounded the Ash. Its medical qualities are such that belief is still said to prevail in the curative powers of the 'Shrew Ash'. Certain it is that in early times young children were 'pushed through an aperture made in the trunk for the cure of childish infirmities'.

The quality of its wood is said to be unsurpassed; and especially in aeroplane manufacture, particularly during the Second World War when the demand for its timber outstripped the supply.

The Ash is not particularly long-lived; its normal span does not extend beyond 200 years. It is generally cut for its timber between fifty and sixty years. No hardwood tree, we are told, repeats itself so vigorously or produces by its winged seeds so many young seedlings.

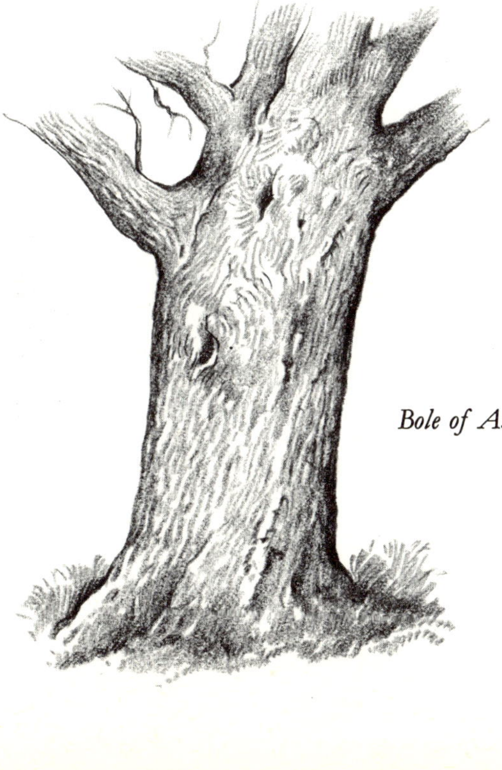

*Bole of Ash*

*Ash*

DESCRIPTION

A well-grown Ash can form a magnificent head and its outline is generally circular in shape. The stout perpendicular trunk is a pale grey colour (hence perhaps its name), evenly furrowed with short vertical fissures.

It has been called a lazy tree, as its leaves appear long after most of the other deciduous trees (except for the Lime and Acacia) and are shed before most of the others in early autumn. These leaves are borne in opposite pairs and are composed of three to eight lance-shaped leaflets, finely serrated and forming a plume-like foliage. In early spring the stoutness of the upturned twigs is very noticeable. The undistinguished flowers appear in May, hanging from the sides of the branches, to be succeeded by clusters of 'keys' which rotate in the wind and speed to earth at considerable distances.

It easily attains a height of 80 feet with a girth of 12 feet, and the branches springing horizontally as well as vertically give the Ash its roughly circular outline.

*Leaves of Ash*

## THE ARTIST'S APPROACH

The Ash will always remain a favourite with painters who discriminate and appreciate the architectural aspect of trees. These qualities are demonstrated in the design of trunk and branch and in the rhythm of the fern-like foliage which responds to the slightest breeze, lifting its graceful arms with their delicate burden of light green leaves. Its lower branches often extend to such a breadth that it is very suitable in a horizontal design. Despite its dense appearance in full summer, the lyrical manner in which the fern-like foliage grows lends itself to the transparent technique of watercolour rather than the plastic nature of oils. A strong pen line with pure washes of transparent colour will achieve the required balance of texture and form.

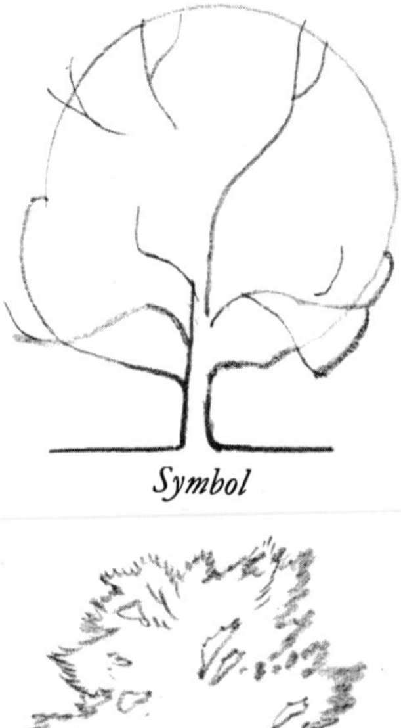

*Symbol*

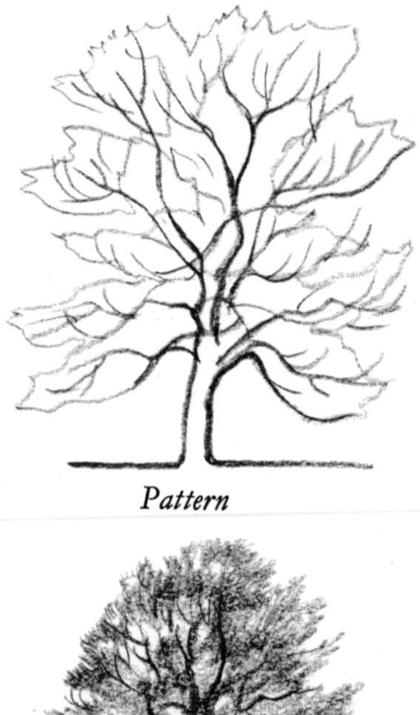

*Pattern*

*Outline*

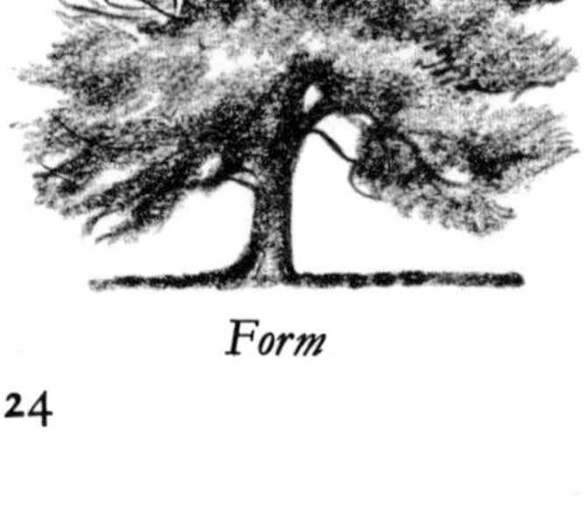

*Form*

*Ash* (*see p.* 21)

*Beech* (*see p. 25*)

# *The Beech*

HISTORY

All the experts now agree that the Beech is indigenous to Britain in spite of the fact that Julius Caesar did not mention it in his reports of the forest trees he found on his first visit to England! It is now said that he did not penetrate far enough into the hinterland, where it is known to have flourished. Remains of the Beech have been discovered in Neolithic deposits in such widely separated counties as Hampshire, Essex, Norfolk, and Buckinghamshire.

There is certainly no question that it has always been regarded as one of the loveliest of our trees, for whatever the season of the year it always looks its best. For some time the forester had little use for it, and were it not for its charm and beauty, it might well have been allowed to die out. Of later years, however, we are told that its timber has been in such a great demand that no tree has been more ruthlessly cut down. Another reason which establishes its right to be preserved is that it is universally recognized as a foster-mother to the growth and upbringing of all other young forest trees—hence its title 'The Mother of Forests'. The Beech, we are told (like some human beings), 'becomes in later life aggressive and overbearing, so that any woodland of mixed trees will be dominated and eventually expelled by the Beech'!

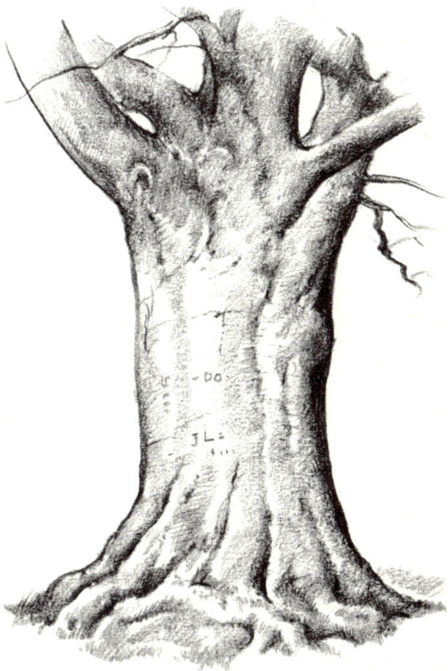

*Bole of Beech*

*Beech*

*Leaves of Beech*

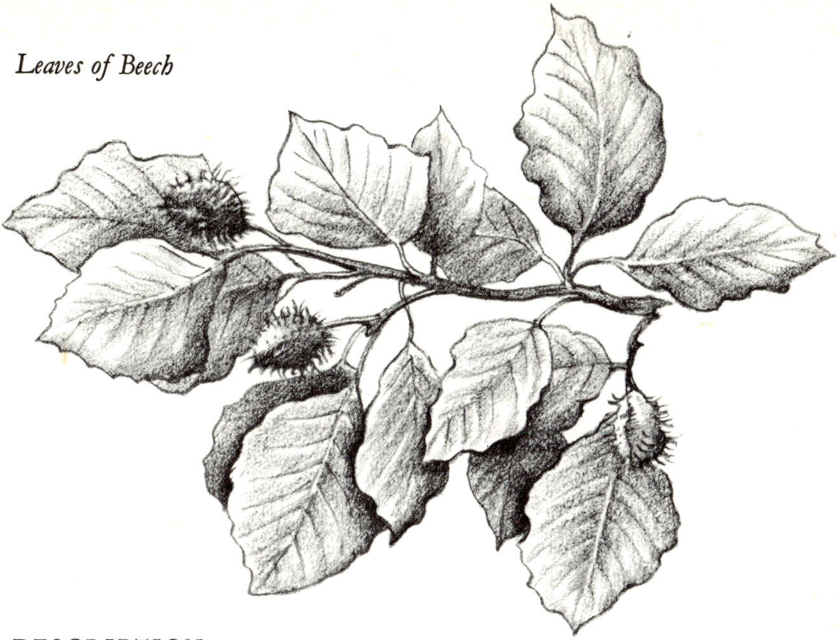

DESCRIPTION

It has a distinctive trunk, being smooth and of a greenish-grey colour. When fissures occur they run horizontally round the bark. The boughs, long and muscular, are flexible and graceful in direction. And even when approaching 300 years of age, the Beech 'keeps its figure' and shows few signs of decay. The roots are often exposed, especially when the surrounding ground has fallen away, as on roadside banks, and like giant 'fingers' they can be seen to grasp the soil with a tenacious grip. With a girth of some 20 feet, the Beech can rise to a height of over 100 feet.

The oval leaves have a glossy surface and a wavy rather than a notched outline. As they are borne alternately they appear to be spread on the branches, thus providing admirable shade, beneath which no grass grows, but only a short moss. Animals such as the deer and fox and rabbit seek shelter in its shade. The small nuts with their furry shells appear in July. In autumn the leaves go from a glossy green to pale yellow, and in October turn to bronze, which enhances the silvery-green hue of the trunk. A beautiful variety is the Copper Beech (shown in colour), a peculiarity of which, in an old tree, is that the leaves revert to a brownish green as autumn approaches.

### THE ARTIST'S APPROACH

The grace and strength of the Beech make it a fitting feature for many landscape subjects. As a 'dry' tree, the trunk and branch construction form lovely designs and offer good examples for careful pencil studies. The Beech can be depicted as a lofty or a spreading tree, and the subtle grey-green of its sinuous trunk with the horizontal layers of sparkling leaves in spring present a truly lovely colour scheme. In autumn the 'sweet' coloration is apt to verge into the 'pretty, pretty'. Generally speaking, the Beech is more easily portrayed as a close-up than in a full-size picture which attempts to include the topmost branches. It is well fitted to the medium of oil, watercolour, or tinted drawing.

*Symbol*

*Pattern*

*Outline*

*Form*

# *The Birch*

HISTORY

The first mention of the origin of the Birch comes from Pliny the Elder, who writing in A.D. 50 says, 'This tree which is meere French and came first out of Fraunce, sheweth wonderful white. . . .' And Shakespeare's poetic warnings about the use of Birch rods for delinquent children dates it sufficiently in history for us to claim it as a naturalized subject of many generations! In Britain the Birch is more widely distributed than any other tree, thriving in almost all soils, and it is always a surprise that a tree fashioned so delicately—has it not won the title as 'The Lady of the Woods'?—should be so tough and hardy. Although it attains a height of 80 feet in America, the average height in the British Isles remains about 50 feet with a girth of 2 to 3 feet. It rarely lives longer than eighty years. It is used extensively for small furniture of all kinds and, if properly treated, makes a good substitute for Mahogany. The Birch can be said to delight both the artist and the timber merchant!

*Bole of Silver Birch*

*Silver Birch*

*Leaves of Silver Birch*

DESCRIPTION

The trunk is specially distinctive because of its habit of shedding its outer layer of bark in horizontal tissue shreds, revealing patches of silvery-white texture which can be seen from a distance.

It can hardly be said to boast boughs, but produces long branches, black and slender, which droop at the extremities and from which the little leaves are borne on long foot-stalks, so that, like those of the Aspen, they flutter at the softest breeze. The leaves are small and diamond-shaped and their edges are doubly toothed. In April the short hanging catkins are first noticeable by their dark crimson colour (as with the Alder). In the early spring, the tree puts out sprays of the lightest foliage, covering the tree with a transparent green gauze or mist. As summer approaches and the leaf grows, the colour deepens to a darkish green which in autumn fades to the palest yellow. Often the main trunk divides from the bole in two or more flexible stems which form a wide crown.

## THE ARTIST'S APPROACH

The artist need not travel very far to enjoy the beauty of a Birch wood. The Londoner indeed need go no farther than Putney Heath. These native plantations are everywhere. As a single tree in a garden, with its characteristic charm of suppleness and shimmering foliage, in roadside groups or in mass formation on heath or common, the Birch makes an immediate appeal to the painter. It combines grace with a quality of firmness, from the sinuous bole to the topmost branches. Furthermore, the texture of the trunk (for which the oil painter may use a palette-knife technique and the watercolour painter may get by the whiteness of the paper) and the wonderful changes of foliage coloration throughout the year, make it one of the most accommodating models in the field of landscape painting.

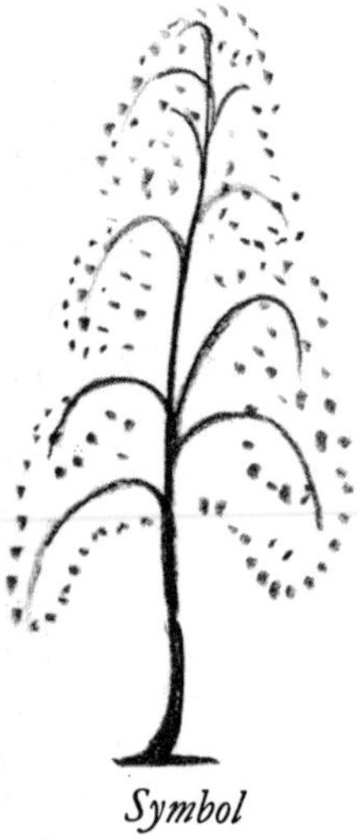
*Symbol*

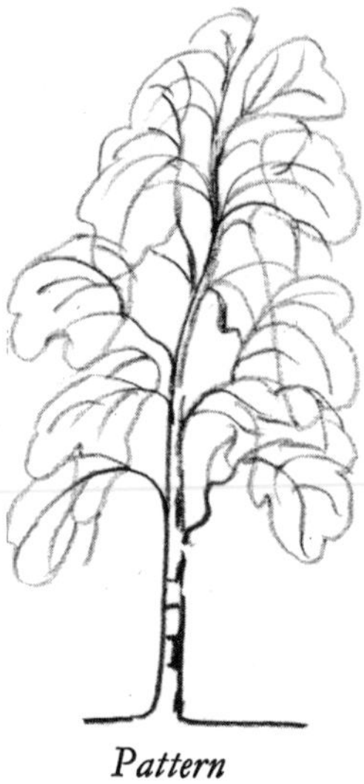
*Pattern*

*Outline*

*Form*

*Silver Birch*

*Spanish Chestnut* (*see p. 33*)

# *The 'Sweet' or 'Spanish' Chestnut*

HISTORY

Because it is sometimes called the 'Spanish' Chestnut, it might be implied that this tree is of foreign origin, but there are a number of arguments in favour of its being a true native of Britain. One is that several places in England take their names from these trees, notably Norwood Chesteney and Chestnut Hill near Sittingbourne; also a number of very old houses contain wood of the Chestnut.

Perhaps it would be safer to call it the 'Sweet' Chestnut, and it is fairly certain that it was planted extensively as a forest tree up to 100 years ago. Since then it has been sadly neglected, except when it is reared for a ten-year crop for Chestnut fencing, which has been in increasing demand in recent years.

The fruit was highly valued for human consumption, especially, we are told, by the Romans, Spaniards, and French; and Evelyn describes the nut as 'a lusty and masculine food for rustics at all times'. It is claimed that the Chestnut has a life span of over 500 years and certainly there remain some splendid specimens today.

*Bole of Spanish Chestnut*

*Spanish Chestnut*

DESCRIPTION

The Sweet Chestnut is luxuriant and majestic. The sturdy perpendicular trunk has a network of deep furrows, which sometimes take a spiral direction, giving the trunk a twisted appearance. It appears taller than it actually is because the trunk diminishes abruptly to form a small crown at a height of about 80 feet. The heavy branches growing out horizontally at first tend to droop downwards, so that the lowest are often only within a few feet of the bole.

The leaves are very striking, some 9 to 10 inches long, elliptical in shape and deeply notched with a highly polished texture. In late July the graceful spiky flowers (up to 6 inches long and notable for their strong and rather sickly scent) make their appearance, and from the base of these the well-known nut is eventually produced. In the autumn the leaves turn pale yellow and then deepen into gold and finally fall to form a thick brown carpet of rich leaf mould.

*Leaves of Spanish Chestnut*

THE ARTIST'S APPROACH

As with so many trees, the Sweet Chestnut appears to the artist's eyes to improve with age. The expression of sturdy strength develops in later life until heaving its ancient form up amongst its neighbours, it proclaims its pictorial lordship over them all with the undisputed right of a patriarch. It is equally impressive without its leaves as the design of trunk and branches can then be properly appreciated, and are noteworthy in your sketch-book. The closer one approaches the tree, the more wealth of character is revealed, not only in the grand twist of the trunk, but in the tenacious roots and muscular tension of the lower boughs. The unusual size and length of the leaves in summer suggest a stylized technique of painting, presenting an opportunity for decorative treatment. At a distance, however, and seen, as it were, 'full length' it is not really possible to include such details and they must be surrendered to its fundamental qualities of height and depth.

*Symbol* *Pattern* *Outline* *Form*

# *The Hornbeam*

HISTORY

Although the Hornbeam has long been accepted as indigenous to Britain, I would say that it is one of the most difficult trees to recognize by anyone except an experienced tree lover. It has a superficial resemblance to the Beech—or Wych Elm—but this is not borne out on closer inspection.

The name is said to derive from the tough or horn-like substance of its 'beams'. Another theory is that it became known as Hornbeam because the horns of bullocks were attached to yokes made from its wood. However this may be, Hornbeam wood is very hard and difficult to 'work', and so is not popular with the carpenter. The Hornbeam grows haphazardly throughout England. In the south it grows here and there and seldom in great numbers, except north and east of London, where in Epping, for example, there still exists a famous forest of Hornbeam trees.

The reason that the trees here are all pollarded (and many date back to 150 to 350 years ago) is thought to be because the branches were cut to provide food for the herds of deer, maintained for hunting purposes.

*Bole of Hornbeam*

*Hornbeam*

*Leaves of Hornbeam*

DESCRIPTION

As the Hornbeam has no strong distinguishing character, it is only on close inspection that it can be correctly identified. For instance, until it divides in manifold branches, the trunk is straightish with irregular vertical fissures (when mature) and is invariably found in form to be elliptical and not round, as tree-trunks usually are. Individual branches have a habit of growing together when they touch in crossing. The leaves resemble those of an Elm. The flowers appear soon after the leaves in April and are succeeded by clusters of small nuts, contained in the bottom of leafy cups. The leaves turn quickly from a dull yellow to a rusty brown and, like the sheltered Oak and Beech, this withered foliage is sometimes retained throughout the winter. The Hornbeam frequently reaches a height of 50 to 60 feet.

Both the literary and artistic world have tended to neglect the Hornbeam because it is a retiring tree with no striking attributes. But in fact it can look quite stately even when it is serving as a hedge in gardens or parks. In winter the construction of the sometimes trumpet-shaped trunk provides excellent studies for pencil or chalk. And when pollarded there is a profusion of branches coming from this. In spring where you have a number of trees growing together the fresh green foliage which mantles the spreading branches presents a variety of tree compositions, the colour and tone of which can be well captured in both oil and watercolour techniques.

A glance at the diagrams will show the difference in construction and habit of growth to the Beech; this is especially distinguishable when growing in isolation in garden or park.

Like many other trees, the Hornbeam makes a better picture when well advanced in years.

*Symbol*

*Pattern*

*Outline*

*Form*

*Hornbeam* *(see p. 37)*

*Black Poplar* (*see p. 41*)

# *The Black Poplar*

HISTORY

Although it is not certain, there seems to be sufficient evidence to consider the Black Poplar as a native of Britain, especially in Wales and wherever there is a moist soil. Its name could well describe the blackness of its bark, particularly of those grown in and around London, but we are told it is so named to distinguish it from the White Poplar, the leaves of which are of a white or greyish down texture on the underside.

While it has been likened to the Lombardy, probably because it has the same sort of leaves, its appearance and habit of growth is entirely dissimilar. Like the Lombardy, however, it shares the same untidy habits and possesses similar 'greedy roots which disturb and starve all plants growing nearby'. Of the many other species of Poplar in this country, from the timber merchant's viewpoint, the Black is the only one whose wood is marketable. It is easy to work and used largely for toy-making and small cabinet-work. Large quantities have also been used for the manufacture of plywood.

*Bole of Black Poplar*

*Black Poplar*

*Leaves of Black Poplar*

DESCRIPTION

Black Poplars are more abundant in London and the Home Counties, springing up in suburban gardens, lining streets, and conspicuous in open spaces and public parks. The stout trunk is generally divided into two long main limbs from which the lesser branches spring at irregular intervals and in wayward directions. It is covered with dark grey bark, heavily corrugated in long vertical fissures. When fully grown the Poplar can reach 60 feet. The scarlet catkins appear in March as it blossoms before leafing; and the effect of red catkins on the leafless branches is very picturesque. The leaves, which vary in size and shape, sometimes heart-shaped, sometimes almost round, are 1 to 4 inches in width. Like the Lombardy and Aspen, the Black Poplar is sensitive to the lightest breeze so that the trunk and branch formation are rarely hidden. Indeed the foliage enhances, like a transparent green haze or sheath, the skeleton construction underneath, investing it with its own peculiar charm and distinction.

Because of its apparent lack of depth in full summer leaf, the Black Poplar is a difficult tree to paint, especially in watercolour. A broad, heavy treatment defeats its ends, while a more meticulous approach can lead to a fussy result.

It is a case of choosing the season rather than looking for any particular specimen. And the Poplar, in my opinion, is a winter rather than a summer tree. The lines of the bare tree are clearly defined and easy to follow. In the right surroundings in the late autumn or very early spring, it offers a variety of pictorial possibilities. It can be legitimately used to heighten the atmospheric effect. Its ungainly growth and stark appearance give it a becoming awkwardness as though it were flinging its arms about in careless gestures. These can be attributes when used to emphasize the uncompromising conditions of a winter morning on the outskirts of some industrial town, and can lend effect to an urban scene lit by the feeble light of an early spring sun.

*Symbol*

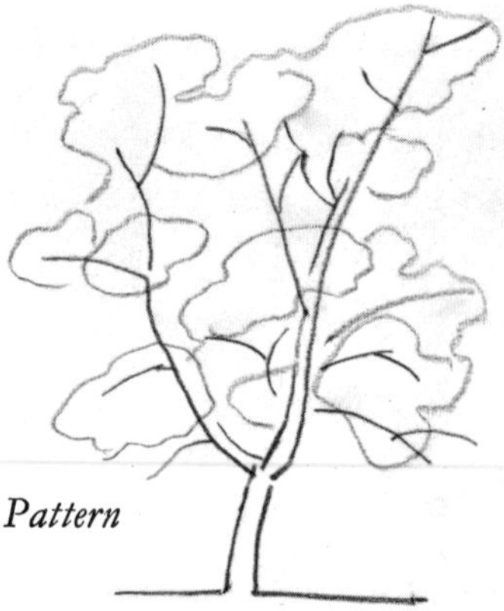

*Pattern*

*Outline*

*Form*

# *The Walnut*

HISTORY

The Walnut is indigenous to such countries as China, Japan, Persia, and the Himalayas. There is a doubt about the exact date of its introduction over here, but it is generally reckoned to be somewhere in the sixteenth century. It was certainly recorded as growing in orchards and along the highways at the end of that century. The contention that the name is a contraction of Walsh-nut—meaning foreign—is no doubt correct. In European countries it was immediately appreciated and extensively cultivated as a timber tree, but more recently it has been cultivated as a fruit tree. Over here it serves both purposes. As wood it is easily worked and takes a beautiful polish. It is a firm favourite as a garden tree, not only for its fruit but as a decorative addition to any lawn.

The ancient adage—'A dog, a wife and a walnut tree, the more you beat them, the better they be'—presumably refers to the manner of harvesting the fruit rather than for encouraging their growth!

*Bole of Walnut*

*Walnut*

*Leaves of Walnut*

DESCRIPTION

The Walnut is lovable and picturesque. It can hardly be called a handsome tree, except for some of the very tall ones, which can reach a height of 60 feet. The majority are of more modest proportions, and their appeal is rather in their distinctive way of growth than in their stature. The stout trunk often divides close to the bole and is usually set at an angle. It is covered with a smooth bark when young, but becomes rugged in age, developing deep vertical fissures.

The branches in the winter can be seen to twist and turn in a wayward fashion, giving the tree an Oriental appearance and permitting plenty of broad spaces, irregular in area, to occur between trunk and main boughs. In full leaf, this construction is obscured by its wealth of foliage. In early spring, first the flowers then the leaf buds appear. The bright green glossy leaves, at first an orange-pink, are peculiar in that their outline is not serrated, as in almost all the leaves of other trees. They generally grow in sprays of five lance-shaped leaflets, in the same way as the Ash and Laburnum. The summer tree is particularly attractive. The fruit, which ripens in October, forms the popular nut.

Perhaps because I have known two Walnut trees within sight of my garden, this tree has a special place in my collection of tree studies. Without its leaves it is a very interesting model to draw, and in summer its warm green foliage, grown in simple, clearly defined masses which are sensitive to the slightest breeze, makes it a suitable subject for painting. Because of the striking manner of growth which increases with age it retains its pictorial virtues even when it can be said to be on its last legs. Indeed, before it was cut down, one tree in particular presented me with a perfect subject; bowed but unbroken, it remained dignified to the end. Its rugged twisted limbs formed a perfect frame beneath which the long low thatch of a farm building gave adequate support to the composition.

*Symbol*

*Pattern*

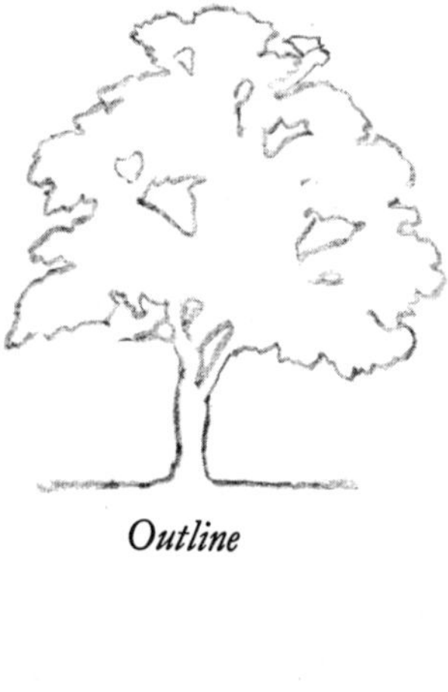

*Outline*

*Form*

*Walnut* (see p. 45)

*Bay-Leaved Willow (see p. 49)*

# *The Willows*

HISTORY

There are so many varieties of the Willow family that it is quite difficult to identify them. It is easy enough when they are nicely labelled in botanical gardens, but when met at random in the countryside even the experts are hard put to it to disentangle the species. There are, to name only a few, the White Willow, the Cricket Bat, the Crack, the Almond-leaved, the Bay-leaved, two or three Sallows, and the Osiers, and in shape and manner of growth they all differ considerably.

The name Willow comes from the Anglo-Saxon, *Welig*, meaning 'pliancy' and 'willingness'. Mention of the tree occurs in the Old Testament—Leviticus 23: '. . . Willows of the brook' in connection with the feast of the Tabernacles, and in Isaiah 44, alluding to the Israelities, 'They shall spring up . . . as Willows by the watercourses.' Indeed they are mainly associated as a river tree. They hail from the temperate regions of the northern hemisphere, and in this country flourish in moist soils and wherever there is water. Rapid in growth, the timber of some kinds, notably the Bedford, is considered most valuable. None of them appear to attain any great age.

*Bole of Bat Willow*

*Pollarded Willow*

DESCRIPTION

Willows vary in height from 3 or 4 feet as a shrub to about 60 feet when fully mature. The trunks are perpendicular and divide in some species into two or three main branches which stem out at wide angles. They are covered with a texture of evenly fissured bark, grey to brownish in colour. The branches are strong, long, flexible, and smooth in texture. The leaves are undivided and either serrated, notched, or plain round the edge, often finished with stipules and varying in shape from arrow-head to round, but mostly elliptical in form. The catkins appear early, in the middle of March.

The easiest to recognize is the Pollarded Willow, which is usually seen along the edges of a waterway and which I have illustrated here.

*Leaves of Bat Willow*

Some people feel that Willows have not ranked high as a subject for artists. I flatly disagree. All the Willows (and there are at least twenty-five different species to choose from) are to be highly recommended in any landscape, particularly those which include water. They fit naturally into such a picture and take their place for the reason that they harmonize so well into the rural scene. Never dramatic, and not majestic enough to dominate a picture, Willows, singly or in groups, either bare of branch—and what beautiful designs they make silhouetted against the sky—or in their full grey-green foliage provide a great variety of shapes for the artist. The Willow is thus wonderfully accommodating to the painter in watercolour or oils, as well as to the graphic artist who works in line and tone.

*Shapes of Willow Trees*

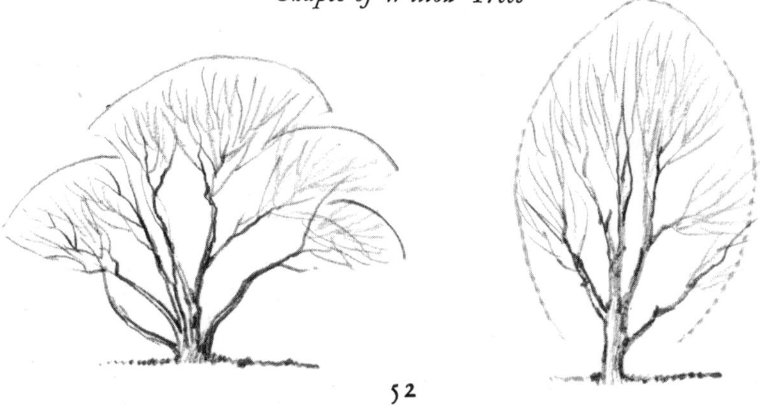

# *The Weeping Willow*

HISTORY

The Weeping Willow is a native of Japan and other parts of Asia, and was introduced into Britain in 1730. We read that the first one was planted in Twickenham by the poet Alexander Pope, and became his favourite tree. It soon became fashionable to plant Weeping Willows, and the cult spread all over Europe until the majority of the gardens and parks included it among their ornamental trees. In warm countries, which it prefers, especially in parts of Chile, the Willow can achieve a substantial height.

*Bole of Weeping Willow*

*Weeping Willow*

*Leaves of Weeping Willow*

DESCRIPTION

The Weeping Willow is one of the easiest of trees to recognize. Although others like the Ash and Elm are made to 'weep', the Willow stands alone from all other trees in its distinctive form and construction. It has been likened to a frozen fountain because when the trunk is completely hidden by silvery leaves, which festoon the long drooping branches, often touching the surrounding earth, it resembles a cascade of water. Actually the shape of the tree varies enormously, but it is only when the wind lifts the graceful branches that glimpses of trunk and main stems are visible.

In the early spring, the Weeping Willow is one of the first to come to life with its rare golden buds which gradually mature into the light, warm green of the full summer leaf. In autumn it reverts to its original amber. It thus preserves its charm throughout the year.

The leaves, in long pendulous sprays and lance-like in shape, are set opposite each other, about a dozen to a branch.

It is one of the most difficult trees to draw or paint because of its regular leaf construction, which gives an almost solid cage-like shape. From its appearance in the 'Willow pattern' of Chinese origin to the famous 'Willow pattern' wall-paper designed by William Morris, the tree has always presented something of a problem to the artist, which only personal experiment can eventually solve. Its 'bone' construction, as it were, can be studied during its dry period, but the true character and poetic charm of the tree can only be portrayed by the discovery of some personal technique. Perhaps a mixture of pen and wash is as sympathetic a medium as any, especially in the setting of a river or lake, and when a breeze disturbs its dense foliage.

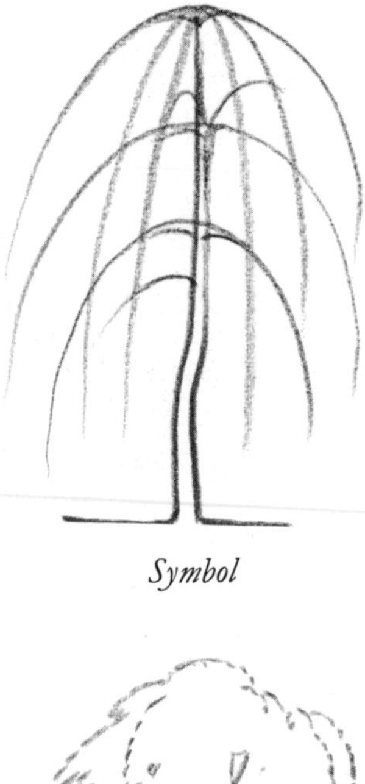

*Symbol*

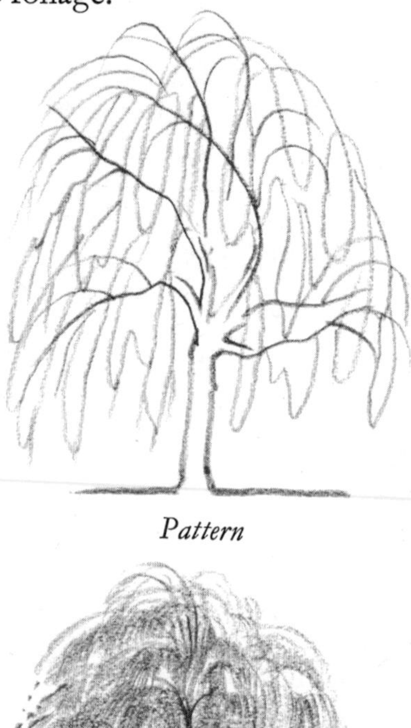

*Pattern*

*Outline*

*Form*

*Weeping Willow* (see p. 53)

*Yew*

# *The Yew*

HISTORY

The Yew shares with our native Oak the honour of being the tree of earliest origin in Great Britain, its history going back well over 2,000 years. (The oldest wooden weapon ever found is a spear of English Yew.) The Yew is steeped in history, much of which is sinister. Woven round its grim character all kinds of superstitions have grown, mostly of illness and death, as it has been considered a tree highly poisonous to man and beast. Its frequent growth in country churchyards, together with its sombre appearance, no doubt contributed to these ancient beliefs and gave rise to its association with death and immortality. It is probable that the Yew tree was planted near churches as a protection and afforded suitable supplies of wood for making bows and spears which for long periods were the national weapons in England. Because of its slow growth, the wood becomes hard and compact and exceedingly prized for its durability, which is sometimes said to be better even than iron for the construction of posts.

*Bole of Yew*

*Yew Tree*

*Leaves of Yew*

DESCRIPTION

The squat appearance of the average Yew can be accounted for by its great width from 25 to 50 feet, which is usually composed of several trunks united together like clustered columns in a cathedral. These are covered with a brittle reddish bark which peels off in irregular patches, somewhat similar to the Plane and Birch trees.

The multiple branches, which spring within a few feet of the bole in a horizontal direction, form an almost solid umbrella, being clad throughout the year with dense masses of evergreen leaves. These 'needles', dark green in texture, are borne in wiry sprays, fern-wise on the branch. In the spring they are tipped with light green 'fingers' of the new growth, and further enlivened by the bright scarlet colour of the cup-like berry.

Although rarely exceeding 25 feet in height, there is to my knowledge a Yew wood in Midhurst, Sussex, formed by four avenues of trees which are reputed to be the tallest in Europe, many rising to a height of 75 to 80 feet and which, in spite of their great age, are still reported to be in good health.

Pictorially the Yew is always happily placed when growing near or against some ancient building. It seems to need the support of some such ageing fabric as provided by a weathered wall or church tower, if only to show off its rugged form and rich muted green foliage, together with the dense pool of shadow that envelops its furrowed bole.

The Yew fits well into a horizontal composition and, like other spreading trees which express their paintable qualities in trunk and lower branch formation, repays a close inspection. For it is only then that its sinuous construction and rich colouring can be properly appraised. It provides ample pictorial material for pen, chalk, or brush—or a mixture of all three: for a combination of media may better depict the Yew than limiting oneself to one medium.

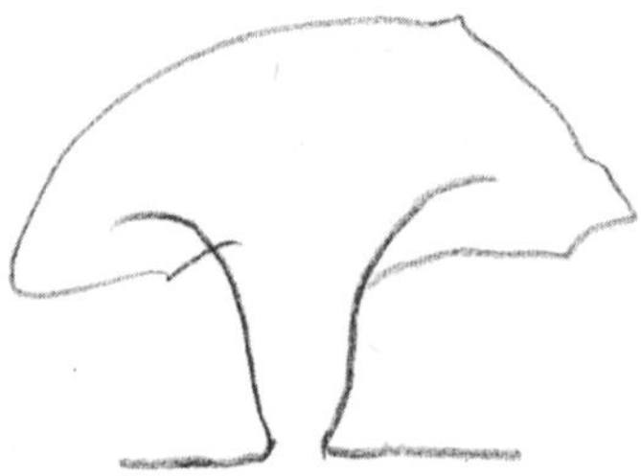

*Symbol*

*Pattern*

*Outline*

*Form*

## *Heights of Trees*

Obviously trees, like people,
grow to varying heights, but it is
interesting to see these heights in relation
to one another. Overleaf I have sketched
the twelve trees in this book
in their relative sizes.

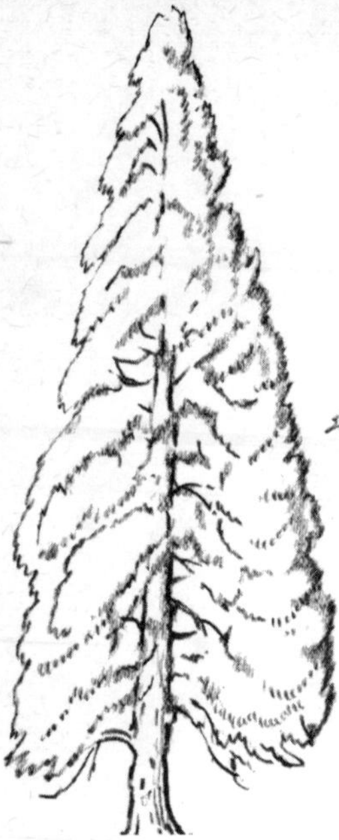

*Wellingtonia*
*100–140 ft.*

*Beech*
*90 ft.*

*Ash*
*80 ft.*

*Hornbeam*
*60 ft.*

*Black Poplar*
*60 ft.*

*Walnut*
*50 ft.*

*Sweet Chestnut*
*60 ft.*

*Silver Birch*
*60 ft.*

*Acacia*
*60 ft.*

*Willow*
*45–50 ft.*

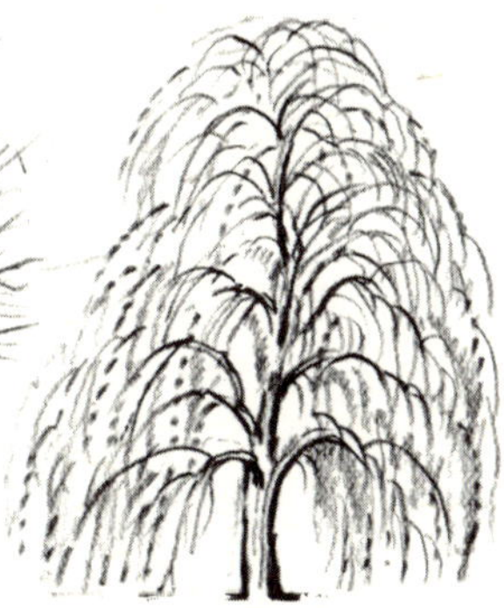

*Weeping Willow*
*40 ft.*

*Yew*
*30–40 ft.*

# *Other Books by Adrian Hill*

WHAT SHALL WE DRAW?

"In this book, as in television programmes, Adrian Hill stimulates the reader in more than just desire for craftsmanship. He asks us to see things as they really are, and then to portray them. In easy style and clear steps, the book unfolds some of the fundamental stages in sketching."—*Health Education Journal*

THE BEGINNER'S BOOK OF OIL PAINTING

"A very practical approach to the subject by a master of the craft. . . . . Throughout this book the reader is encouraged to be himself and to try his own experiment. . . ."—*The Schoolmaster*

THE BEGINNER'S BOOK OF WATERCOLOUR PAINTING

"The information given, whether it concerns brushes, colours, equipment or technique, is always absolutely sound, as is his insistence on a personal approach. The illustrations are a joy."

*The Schoolmaster*

KNOWING AND DRAWING TREES, Books 1 and 2

"Anyone with an appreciation of natural beauty will find this small though beautifully produced volume a delight to possess. Adrian Hill has the technical skill of a first-rate draughtsman plus the selective perception and good taste of a first-rate artist."

*Art News and Review*

FACES AND FIGURES

"Full of extremely valuable practical hints to the aspiring craftsman, and the text is embellished by excellent illustrations and diagrams." —*London Head Teacher*

SKETCHING AND PAINTING INDOORS

"This is the sort of book which immediately sends the young artist to his sketch book."—*Art and Craft Education*